Mucus Timeline

ca. 460–ca. 370 BCE
Greek physician Hippocrates popularizes the idea that human health is based on the four humors, one of which is phlegm.

1785
King Louis XVI of France issues a decree banning anyone from carrying a handkerchief larger than his.

1924
Kleenex® introduces the first disposable facial tissues.

750 CE
In ancient Rome, it becomes customary to say "God bless you" after someone sneezes.

1921
Alexander Fleming discovers that mucus contains the bacteria-killing substance lysozyme.

900s
Arab scholar Ibn Fadlan describes the Viking morning ritual of blowing one's nose into a bowl of water.

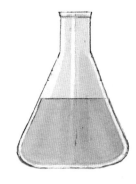

1972
The neti pot, which originated in ancient India, goes on sale in the United States.

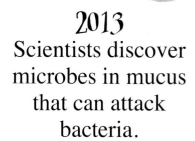

1932
Polish physician Alfred Laskiewicz promotes nasal irrigation to deal with excess mucus.

2013
Scientists discover microbes in mucus that can attack bacteria.

1938
American physician Dorothy H. Anderson identifies the disease cystic fibrosis.

2015
Scientists discover a method of repairing damaged mucins—the most important components of mucus.

1999
Scientists discover the body's trigger for uncontrolled mucus production.

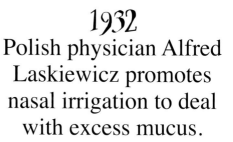

Mucus in Our Bodies

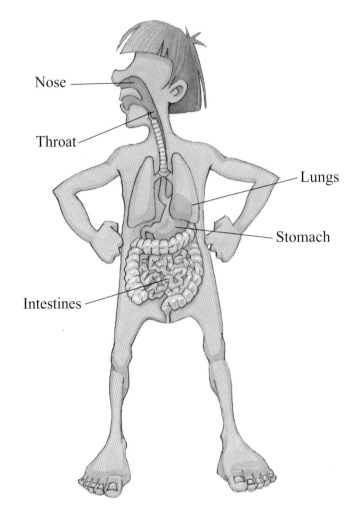

Nose

Throat

Lungs

Stomach

Intestines

Snot is a sticky, slimy, runny substance produced in our noses. It is a form of mucus. Boogers are dried nasal mucus (mucus that forms in our noses). We produce mucus in lots of other places besides our noses, including our throat and lungs (where it's called phlegm), and our stomach and intestines (where it's simply called mucus). This book will focus on the different types of mucus produced in our bodies. We will take a look at how some animals use mucus, too.

Author:

Alex Woolf studied history at Essex University, in England. He is the author of over 60 books for children, many of them on historical topics. They include *You Wouldn't Want to Live Without Books!, You Wouldn't Want to Live Without Money!,* and *You Wouldn't Want to Live Without Vegetables!*

Artist:

David Antram was born in Brighton, England, in 1958. He studied at Eastbourne College of Art and then worked in advertising for 15 years before becoming a full-time artist. He has illustrated many children's nonfiction books.

Series creator:

David Salariya was born in Dundee, Scotland. He has illustrated a wide range of books and has created and designed many new series for publishers in the UK and overseas. David established The Salariya Book Company in 1989. He lives in Brighton with his wife, illustrator Shirley Willis, and their son, Jonathan.

Editor: **Jacqueline Ford**

Editorial Assistant: **Mark Williams**

PAPER FROM

SUSTAINABLE FORESTS

Published in Great Britain in 2017 by
The Salariya Book Company Ltd
25 Marlborough Place, Brighton BN1 1UB

ISBN-13: 978-0-531-22459-5 (lib. bdg.) 978-0-531-22488-5 (pbk.)

All rights reserved.
Published in 2017 in the United States
by Franklin Watts
An imprint of Scholastic Inc.

A CIP catalog record for this book is available from the Library of Congress.

Printed and bound in Heyuan, China.
Printed on paper from sustainable sources.
Reprinted in MMXX.
2 3 4 5 6 7 8 9 10 R 25 24 23 22 21 20

You Wouldn't Want to Live Without™

Boogers!

Written by
Alex Woolf

Illustrated by
David Antram

Series created by
David Salariya

Franklin Watts®
An Imprint of Scholastic Inc.

Contents

Introduction

ave you ever wondered why our bodies make mucus? Without it, the insides of our bodies would be very dry, and we would find it hard to digest our food. We would also quickly become sick, because mucus protects us from dirt in the air that we breathe. Things might smell different, too. Scientists believe that chemicals in mucus catch smells and send them to odor receptors in the nose.

But what exactly is mucus? Is it the same thing as snot? And why do you produce more of it when you have a cold? We'll answer all these questions and more in this book. We'll also look at some of the things animals do with their mucus (you'll be amazed and slightly revolted!). You might find mucus a bit yucky, but you really wouldn't want to live without it!

What Is Mucus?

Mucus is a slimy substance produced by humans and animals. It's mostly made of water, but also contains salt, tissue cells, and chemicals called mucins. Mucus is secreted (produced) by a thin layer of tissue called the mucous membrane. The mucous membrane lines the parts of the body that lead to the outside. That includes the insides of the mouth and nose, the sinuses (hollow spaces in the front of the skull), throat, lungs, and digestive system. Mucus protects these surfaces and prevents them from drying out. It's like the oil in an engine, keeping everything moist, lubricated, and running smoothly. Without it, the engine would seize up.

Mucus is like the oil in the engine.

I think this one's got too much oil.

WHY IS IT STICKY? Mucus contains mucins, which are a bit like long strands of sticky spaghetti. Like spaghetti, mucins get tangled up with each other. That's why mucus is sticky.

That's a lot of mucus!

What is it?

Not sure.

HOW MUCH? The average person produces and swallows around 4 to 6.25 cups (1 to 1.5 liters) of mucus every day! Most of it trickles down your throat without you even noticing.

SNOT AND PHLEGM. We call mucus from our noses snot. The mucus we cough up from our lungs is phlegm.

How Does Mucus Protect Us?

In addition to keeping your insides moist, mucus also protects you. The air you breathe in contains potentially harmful things like dust, dirt, germs, and pollen. If these things made it all the way to your lungs, they might make you sick. Your lungs could become irritated or infected, making it hard to breathe. The mucus that lines your airways stops this from happening. Because the mucus is sticky and thick, it traps the dirt, similar to how a strip of flypaper traps flies. The mucus keeps the impurities in your nose and out of your lungs.

Dealing With Dirt

1. The walls of your air passages are lined with tiny hairs called cilia. These are coated with mucus. Any dirt you breathe in is captured by the mucus.

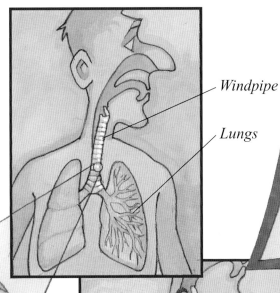

Windpipe

Lungs

To avoid spreading germs, always cover your nose and mouth with the inside of your arm when you cough or sneeze.

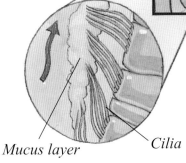

Mucus layer

Cilia

2. The cilia move in a sweeping motion. This sends the mucus back up toward your throat.

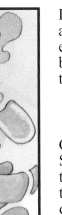

Esophagus

3. You swallow the mucus and any germs are taken into your stomach rather than your lungs. Acids in your stomach kill the germs.

Stomach

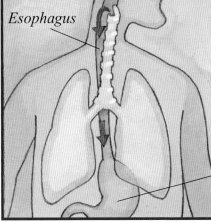

DEFENSE. Mucus contains a special chemical called an enzyme that attacks invading bacteria by breaking down their cell walls.

COUGHS AND SNEEZES. Sometimes, the mucus and the cilia can't keep up with all the invaders, so the body uses different defenses: coughs and sneezes.

9

What Are Boogers and Snot?

Boogers are dried nasal mucus (mucus that forms in the nose). Nasal mucus (or snot) is produced by glands called goblet cells in your nasal passages. How does it become dry? When people breathe in, especially during the winter, they inhale dry air. That's one way that boogers form. They can also form when nasal mucus traps particles in the air. The mucus dries around the particle and hardens, a bit like a pearl forming around a grain of sand in an oyster. Capturing particles is what mucus is supposed to do. So having boogers just proves that your nose is working well.

SNOT COLOR CHART. The color of your snot can tell you a lot about your health. Check out this chart.

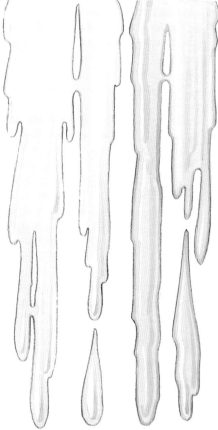

Nose mucus can be hard and dry...those are boogers!

When nose mucus is gooey and slimy, that's snot.

WHITE SNOT. You are congested: Inflamed blood vessels in the nose are slowing the flow of snot, so it loses moisture.

YELLOW SNOT. You have a cold: White blood cells are rushing to the site of the infection.

Make your own fake snot:
- Fill half a cup with boiling water.
- Add 3 teaspoons of gelatin, then stir.
- Add ¼ cup of corn syrup, then stir.
- Let it cool to form slimy, sticky snot.

PHLEGM is a mixture of mucus, saliva, and white blood cells. It's produced by the lower airways such as the windpipe and the lungs. You don't normally notice phlegm until you get sick and you cough it up.

GREEN SNOT.
Your immune system is fighting back: The mucus is thick with dead white blood cells, turning the snot green.

PINK OR RED SNOT.
Blood vessels in your nose have broken, maybe from too much rubbing, blowing, or picking.

BROWN SNOT.
You have probably inhaled some dirt.

BLACK SNOT.
You may have a serious fungal infection. Seek medical attention.

Where Else Do We Produce Mucus?

We mostly think about mucus as snot and phlegm, but other parts of our body produce mucus, too. For example, when we wake up in the mornings, we often find crusty stuff in the corners of our eyes. We call this sleep, but the scientific name for it is gound, and it contains mucus. The mucus in gound is produced by a mucous membrane called the conjunctiva that covers the front of the eye and the inside of the eyelids. Mucus is also produced in our sinuses and within our mouths.

You slept for twelve hours!

That explains all this gound!

A sinus infection, or sinusitis, happens when sinuses become blocked with mucus. Bacteria can grow there, causing infection.

GOUND is made up of a mixture of dust, blood cells, skin cells, and mucus. We produce gound all the time, but during the day it gets washed away when we shed tears or blink.

SINUSES are hollow spaces in the bones of our face, lined with mucous membranes. The mucus drains out of the sinuses into the nose.

MOUTH MUCUS. If your mouth didn't produce mucus, it would become very dry, making it almost impossible to eat your food.

13

Does Mucus Help Us Digest Food?

Thanks to mucus, we can digest even the toughest army rations!

Mucus plays a big part in our digestion. In fact, mucous membrane lines almost our complete digestive tract—the long system of tubes and organs that lead from our mouths to our rear ends. The mucus in our mouths mixes with saliva to start the digestive process by helping to break down food. Mucus, being slippery, eases the passage of food as it passes through the system. It also provides a protective layer that prevents tissues from being scratched or damaged by food.

Digestive System

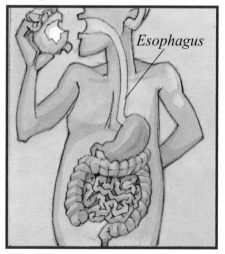

Esophagus

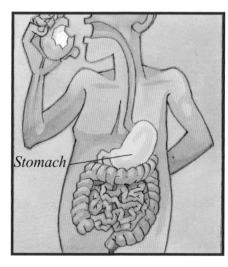

Stomach

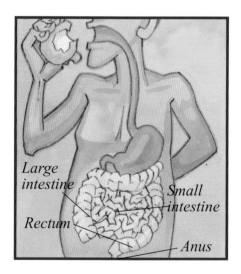

Large intestine

Small intestine

Rectum

Anus

1. ESOPHAGUS. Some mucus is produced by the walls of the esophagus—that's the food pipe that carries food from the mouth to the stomach.

2. STOMACH. A layer of thick mucus lines the wall of the stomach to protect it from the acids that break down the food.

3. INTESTINES. Mucus also coats the inside of our intestines, protecting our guts from infection by bacteria. Some mucus even ends up in our poop.

How It Works

If the stomach's mucus barrier is interfered with, acid attacks the stomach lining, causing an ulcer. Ulcers can occur if a certain type of bacterium infects the stomach, or if people take too much of aspirin-type pain relievers.

PROTECTION. Without the layer of mucus that lines the stomach, the stomach would eat itself! The digestive juices produced in the stomach contain enough acid to burn a hole through your stomach wall.

Sounds dangerous in there!

Rumble!

Too Much of a Good Thing?

Sometimes the mucus layer in your airways lets something slip by, or it is overwhelmed by the amount of particles inhaled. The invading particles might be bacteria or a virus that could give you an infection. Or they might be an allergen like pollen that will irritate your lungs. Your body reacts by producing more mucus to attack the invaders. Normally, mucus is runny and clear. But when fighting germs, your body produces mucus that is thicker, and its color may change to white, yellow, or green.

Surely she can't produce any more!

A cold begins when a virus attaches to the lining of your nose or throat, which become inflamed. Your immune system attacks the virus with white blood cells and lots of mucus.

ALLERGIES. When your body is attacked by an allergen like pollen or ragweed, white blood cells release a substance called histamine, which causes sneezing, itching, and a runny nose.

CYSTIC FIBROSIS. People with this disease produce mucus that is thick and gooey. The cilia can't move the mucus up to the throat and it gets stuck, making it hard to breathe. Special machines called nebulizers help to thin the mucus and make it easier to cough up.

SPICY FOOD. Sometimes your nose runs when you eat hot or spicy food. The mucus is usually quite watery. This reaction is called gustatory rhinitis.

17

How Can We Get Rid of Mucus?

It's never pleasant when your body produces lots of mucus—especially the thicker kind. You feel all stuffed up, food seems to lose its flavor, and no one can understand you when you speak! Blowing your nose doesn't seem to help either. All that does is inflame the blood vessels in your nose. Nights can be especially uncomfortable, because congestion is often worse when you're lying down. So what can you do? There are medicines you can take, or you can use a device called a neti pot to flush out your nose.

What cloud?

That clowd is very fuddy!

18

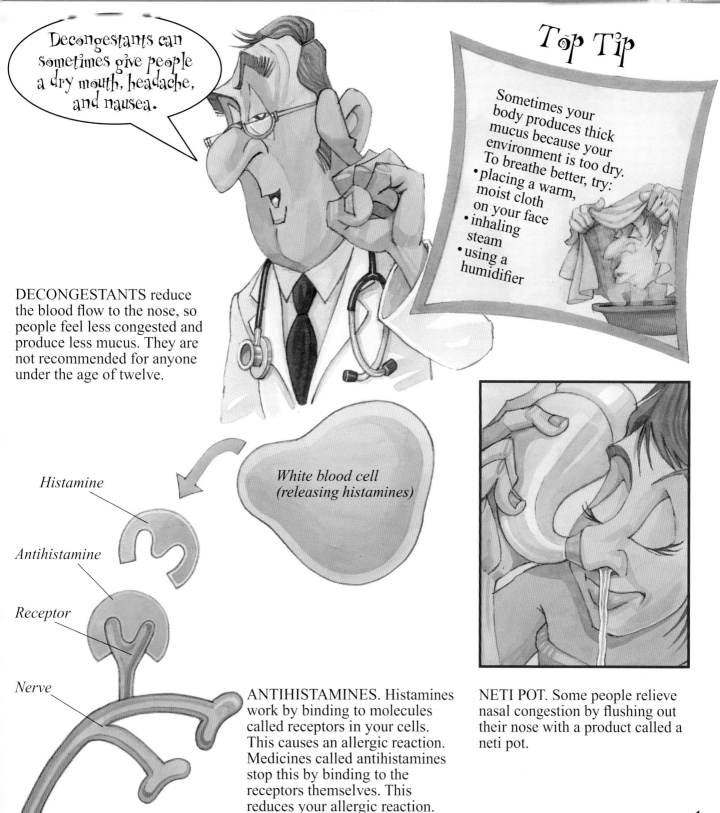

Decongestants can sometimes give people a dry mouth, headache, and nausea.

Top Tip

Sometimes your body produces thick mucus because your environment is too dry. To breathe better, try:
• placing a warm, moist cloth on your face
• inhaling steam
• using a humidifier

DECONGESTANTS reduce the blood flow to the nose, so people feel less congested and produce less mucus. They are not recommended for anyone under the age of twelve.

Histamine

Antihistamine

Receptor

Nerve

White blood cell (releasing histamines)

ANTIHISTAMINES. Histamines work by binding to molecules called receptors in your cells. This causes an allergic reaction. Medicines called antihistamines stop this by binding to the receptors themselves. This reduces your allergic reaction.

NETI POT. Some people relieve nasal congestion by flushing out their nose with a product called a neti pot.

Why Do Slugs and Snails Produce Mucus?

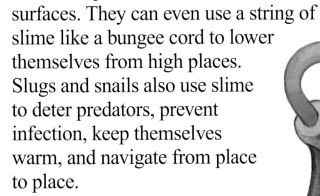

You've probably seen the silvery trails of slime produced by slugs and snails. It turns out that the slime these creatures produce is a kind of mucus, and it's incredibly useful. It coats their bodies, keeping them from drying out in the Sun. It helps them to move around and climb vertical surfaces. They can even use a string of slime like a bungee cord to lower themselves from high places. Slugs and snails also use slime to deter predators, prevent infection, keep themselves warm, and navigate from place to place.

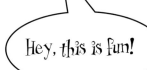

Hey, this is fun!

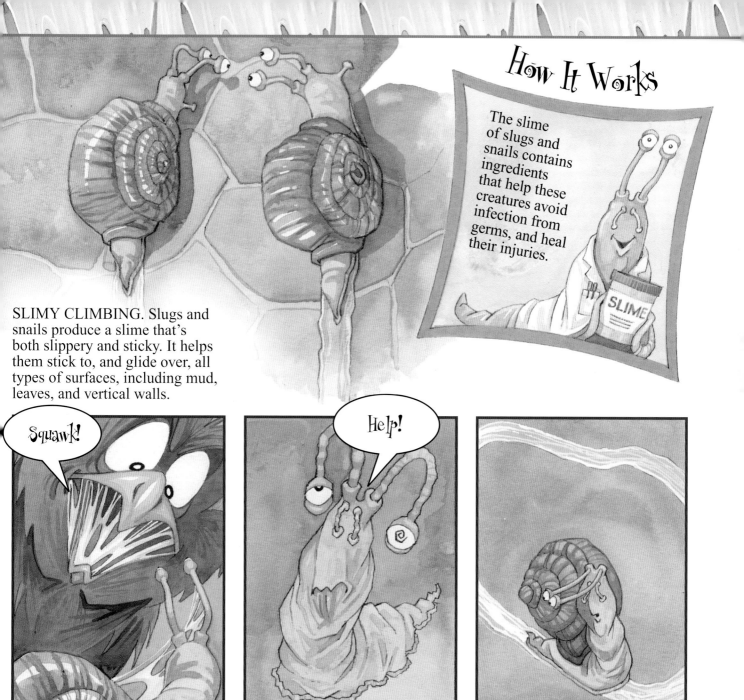

How It Works

The slime of slugs and snails contains ingredients that help these creatures avoid infection from germs, and heal their injuries.

SLIME

SLIMY CLIMBING. Slugs and snails produce a slime that's both slippery and sticky. It helps them stick to, and glide over, all types of surfaces, including mud, leaves, and vertical walls.

Squawk!

Help!

NASTY TASTE. Slugs and snails coat themselves in awful-tasting mucus, so that birds don't eat them. Those birds that do decide to take a peck will find the thick mucus gums up their beaks.

SLIME SHORTAGE. If a slug didn't have slime, it would have trouble moving and it would soon shrivel up and die.

FOLLOW THAT TRAIL. Slugs and snails follow their own trails, or those made by others, to help them locate food or a mate, or to find their way home.

21

What Animals Use Mucus for Defense?

Some animals use mucus to defend themselves against predators. One of the most extraordinary examples of this is an eel-like creature called the hagfish. If a predator such as a shark tries to eat a hagfish, the hagfish shoots out a load of jellylike slime that can clog up the attacker's mouth and gills. The slime contains mucus as well as very strong, silky fibers. The fibers are up to 6 inches (15 centimeters) long and hold the slime together in a big gooey web. The hagfish has no jaws, so its slime serves as a valuable form of self-defense.

Take that!

Yuck! That does not look safe to eat!

OPOSSUM. If an opossum feels threatened, it falls to the ground, foams at the mouth, and produces a horrible, smelly green mucus from its rear end. This usually persuades predators that the opossum is dead.

INK DEFENSE. If an octopus or squid is being chased, it releases a cloud of dark-colored liquid to distract its predator, allowing it to escape. The liquid contains mucus and a pigment called melanin.

If a snake grabs a salamander in its mouth, the salamander produces a thick, sticky mucus. The snake can't close its mouth, so the salamander wriggles free.

Why don't I have any friends?

SMELLY BACKPACK. The larva of the cereal leaf beetle covers its back in a layer of its own mucus and poop to make itself unappetizing to predators.

SLIPPERY FROGS. The North American wood frog is preyed on by snakes and birds. But the mucus that covers its skin is so slimy, the frog often manages to slip away.

23

What Animals Use Mucus for Shelter?

Can you imagine sleeping in a bed of your own mucus? That's what the parrotfish does. Every night, before it goes to sleep, the parrotfish burps out and covers itself with a layer of slimy mucus. Why does it do this? Scientists aren't exactly sure, but they think it's to protect itself from parasites. During the day, these parasites are removed by cleaner fish. But at night, when the cleaner fish sleep, the parrotfish must build itself a slimy sleeping bag so it can sleep safely without being bitten. It's similar to the way we would use a mosquito net.

FROGS. Some frogs build themselves cocoons made of layers of dead skin and mucus to retain moisture during hot, dry weather.

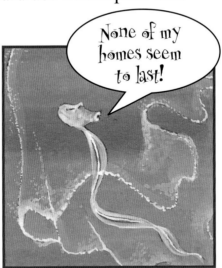

None of my homes seem to last!

I can sleep in my cocoon for up to two years.

MUCUS HOUSES. Tiny sea creatures called larvaceans live in nets spun from their own mucus. They catch falling organic particles in the nets for food. The nets quickly get clogged up, so they have to keep building more.

AFRICAN LUNGFISH. This eel-like fish lives in shallow waters. In the hot summer months it sleeps in burrows of dry mud beneath stream beds. It does this by wrapping itself up in a mucus cocoon.

How Else Do Animals Use Their Mucus?

Mucus is an amazing substance, and creatures use it in many different ways. They use it to move, hunt, stay clean, breathe, and keep cool. Some animals even feed it to their young. The discus fish of the Amazon basin, for example, produce a special kind of mucus just after their fry (baby fish) have hatched. For the next three weeks, the fry nibble the mucus from their parents' skin. During that time, the mucus changes what it is made of to give the fry the nutrition they need.

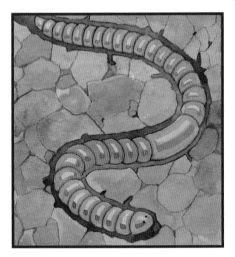

Time for a cleanup!

I must make more mucus!

TUNNEL BUILDERS. Many earthworms produce mucus that helps them move through the soil. With some burrowing earthworms, the mucus hardens around the walls of their tunnels to prevent them collapsing.

CORALS create a layer of sticky mucus around them, which they use to protect themselves from sediment. When too much sediment collects on the mucus, they shed the mucus layer and create a new one.

KEEPING COOL. In hot, dry weather, frogs produce more mucus to trap more moisture on their skin so they can stay cool and moist. Some frogs build up layers of dried mucus for this purpose.

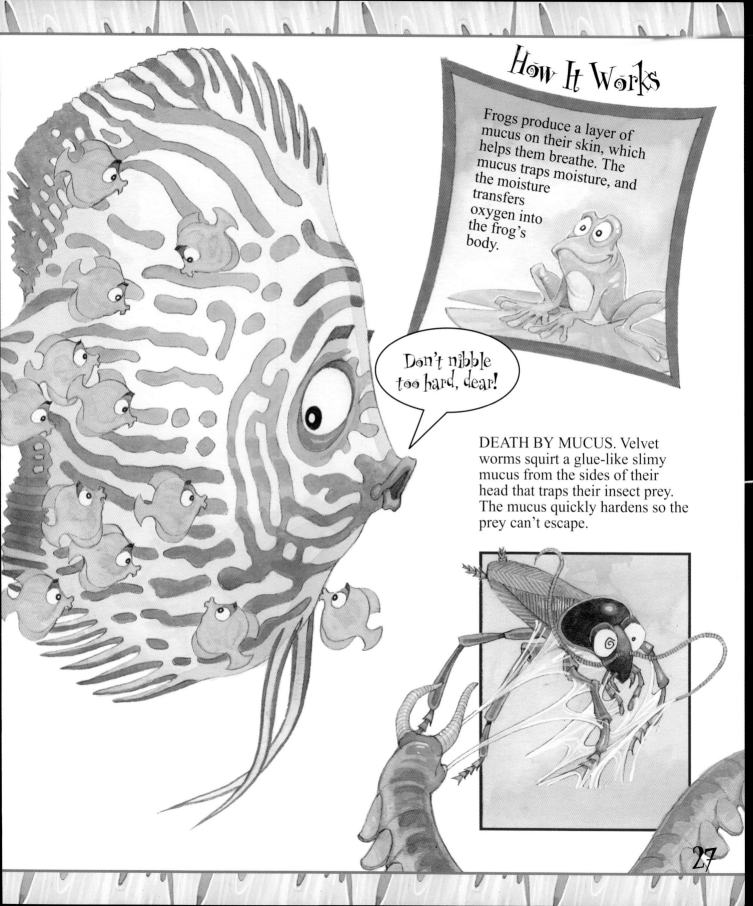

Frogs produce a layer of mucus on their skin, which helps them breathe. The mucus traps moisture, and the moisture transfers oxygen into the frog's body.

Don't nibble too hard, dear!

DEATH BY MUCUS. Velvet worms squirt a glue-like slimy mucus from the sides of their head that traps their insect prey. The mucus quickly hardens so the prey can't escape.

Is Mucus Useful to Us?

For centuries, people have been using snail and slug slime for medical treatments. In ancient Greece, it was used to treat skin conditions and stomach ulcers. The slime was made into a syrup to soothe a cough. Slug slime contains an anesthetic, and may have been used in a Native American cure for toothaches. In the 1980s, Chilean snail breeders noticed that skin wounds healed quickly with no scars after they had handled snails. Today, snail slime is used as an ingredient by some cosmetic manufacturers. They claim it can treat acne and scarring, and reduce wrinkles. So, with all the amazing uses we have for mucus, you really wouldn't want to live without it!

That's gratitude for you!

WART CURE. According to a traditional cure, rub a live slug on a wart, then impale the slug on a thorn. As the slug dries out and dies, the wart will disappear.

WHALE MUCUS. The stuff a whale spouts out of its blow hole is actually lung mucus. Scientists are planning to use aerial drones to collect this, because it can tell them a lot about the whale's stress levels and health.

That flying thing is really stressing me out!

What's the glue made of?

You don't want to know.

SLUG GLUE. When slugs need to cling to an object, they can produce a very sticky kind of mucus. Now, scientists are researching the possibility of using this powerful natural glue for stitching up wounds.

28

This should make me look young again!

Top Tip

Avoid handling wild snails. These creatures often carry diseases.

MARVELOUS MUCUS keeps our insides moist and our bodies free of disease. And now scientists are discovering some amazing uses for animal mucus, including possibly improving the quality of our skin.

Glossary

Allergen A substance that causes an allergic reaction.

Anesthetic A drug that numbs pain.

Bacteria (singular: **bacterium**) A type of microorganism, some of which can cause disease.

Cilia (singular: **cilium**) A microscopic hairlike structure found on the surface of certain cells.

Cocoon Something that envelops a creature in order to protect it.

Congested Blocked with mucus so that breathing is difficult.

Cystic fibrosis A disease that leads to the production of abnormally thick mucus, causing infection and blockage of the lungs and intestines.

Esophagus The muscular tube that takes food from the throat down to the stomach.

Fungal infection Infection caused by fungi—a kingdom of organisms, some of which can cause disease.

Gelatin A virtually colorless and tasteless substance made from animal tissue and used in food preparation and in glue.

Humidifier A device for keeping the atmosphere in a room moist.

Humor During medieval times, one of the four main fluids of the body: blood, phlegm, yellow bile (called choler), and black bile (called melancholy).

Immune system The organs and processes of the body that provide resistance to infection and poisons.

Inflamed (describing a part of the body) reddened, swollen, hot, and often painful, usually as a result of injury or infection.

Lubricate Minimize friction and allow smooth movement.

Mucous membrane A thin layer of

tissue that produces mucus.

Nasal Relating to the nose.

Nasal irrigation The practice of flushing mucus and other debris out of the nasal cavity.

Neti pot A device used for nasal irrigation as a way to relieve congestion.

Organic Made of living matter.

Parasite An organism that lives in or on another organism (its host) and takes nutrients at the host's expense.

Particle A tiny piece of matter.

Phlegm A thick mucus produced by the mucous membrane in the lungs and air passages, produced in large quantities during a cold.

Pigment The natural coloring of animal or plant tissue.

Pollen A fine powdery substance produced by flowers and some other plants.

Sediment Particles carried by water currents that settle on the ocean floor.

Ulcer An open sore on an internal surface of the body caused by a break in the mucous membrane.

White blood cell A colorless cell that circulates in the blood and body fluids and is involved in fighting off foreign substances and disease.

Windpipe The air passage from the throat to the lungs.

Index

Top Animal Users of Mucus

1. Ribbon worms produce a slippery mucus that covers their bodies and protects them from the mud and rocks of the ocean floor. It also makes it very hard for predators to get a grip on them.

2. Snails make a dried lid of mucus over the mouths of their shells, which seals them in for the cold winter months.

3. The vampire squid has a strange way of eating. It grabs particles of sinking organic matter with a long stringlike appendage up to eight times the length of its body. It then envelops the particles in mucus, produced by the suckers on its tentacles, and stuffs the globs of mucus and prey into its mouth.

4. The disco clam is so named because it creates flashes of light to draw in its prey. When the prey comes close, the clam releases poisonous mucus to kill it. These flashes may also help ward off the clam's predators.

5. Glowworm larvae living in New Zealand caves lure their prey by dangling silk threads beaded with sticky mucus from the cave ceiling. When a moth or snail gets trapped in the slimy threads, the glowworm pulls it up to the ceiling and eats it.

6. Violet snails are sea snails that surf the ocean on rafts made from their own mucus. They produce the mucus from their foot. It hardens quickly to create an air-filled floating raft, a bit like bubble wrap.

7. Poison dart frogs produce a sticky mucus, so that their newly hatched tadpoles can stick to their backs during the long and dangerous climb into the rainforest canopy. Once there, the adults drop the tadpoles in pools of water that form in the leaves of large plants.

The Heroic Hagfish

The hagfish is not the most glamorous of creatures. It's jawless, spineless, and it dines on dead animals on the ocean floor. Yet its slime is one of the most incredible substances in nature, and it may be one reason why the hagfish has survived for 500 million years.

Stretchy Threads

When a hagfish is attacked by a predator, it produces slime from glands running along the side of its body. The slime is made up of mucus and very thin, strong, and stretchy threads. The threads are 100 times thinner than a human hair, yet 10 times stronger than nylon. They are arranged in tightly coiled bundles called skeins. When the skeins come into contact with seawater, the glue holding them together dissolves, causing them to quickly unravel, turning a teaspoon of slime into a bucketful of it in seconds. This must make for a very nasty surprise for a predator!

Synthetic Slime

Scientists would like to exploit the incredible qualities of hagfish slime to create new, superstrong, stretchy materials. These could be used to create a whole range of useful things, including pantyhose, sports clothing, food packaging, bandages, airbags, bungee ropes, and bulletproof vests. But hagfish do not respond well to being farmed and will not breed in captivity. So, scientists are trying instead to produce a synthetic version of the slime in the laboratory.

Did You Know?

- Alexander Fleming discovered bacteria-killing lysozyme by accident when a drop of mucus from his nose dripped into a dish of bacteria.

- Ancient Greek and medieval physicians believed that too much phlegm makes a person phlegmatic—in other words, lacking in emotion.

- "Blennophobia" means a fear of slime.

- The *Octochaetus multiporus* earthworm of New Zealand squirts a bright orange-yellow mucus that glows in the dark!

- The green color of snot is caused by the presence of white blood cells called neutrophils. An average human adult can produce up to 100 billion neutrophils in a day.

- The English town of Nottingham got its name from an Anglo-Saxon chieftain named Snot. The town was originally called Snotengaham (meaning "homestead of Snot's people"). When the Normans took control in 1086, they dropped the "s" from the town's name.

- Snails use up about a third of their energy producing mucus. They often save on energy by deliberately following existing slime trails.